Gretchen Bitterlin
Dennis Johnson
Donna Price
Sylvia Ramirez
K. Lynn Savage, Series Editor

Ventures Transitions

TEACHER'S MANUAL

CAMBRIDGE
UNIVERSITY PRESS

CAMBRIDGE
UNIVERSITY PRESS

32 Avenue of the Americas, New York, NY 10013-2473, USA

Cambridge University Press is part of the University of Cambridge.

It furthers the University's mission by disseminating knowledge in the pursuit of education, learning and research at the highest international levels of excellence.

www.cambridge.org
Information on this title: www. cambridge.org/9780521186155

First published 2011
3rd printing 2014

Printed in the United States of America.

A catalog record for this publication is available from the British Library.

ISBN 978-0-521-18613-1 Student's Book and Audio CD
ISBN 978-0-521-18614-8 Workbook
ISBN 978-0-521-18615-5 Teacher's Manual

Cover photography credits: Front (tl) Andrew Zarivny/Shutterstock; (tr) Stuart Monk/Shutterstock; (r) Gary D Ercole/ Photolibrary/Getty Images; (cr) Sam Kolich; (br) Nathan Maxfield/iStockphoto; (c) Monkey Business Images/Shutterstock; (bl) Alistair Forrester Shankie/iStockphoto; (cl) ML Harris/Iconica/Getty Images; (l) Mark Lewis/Digital Vision/Getty Images. Back (tc) cloki/Shutterstock; (br) gualtiero boffi/Shutterstock.

Book design: Adventure House, NYC
Layout services: Page Designs International

Contents

To the teacher

What is *Transitions*?

Transitions is a ten-unit course designed for students who have successfully completed *Ventures* Level 4 or who have tested out of the National Reporting System high-intermediate level. Students using *Transitions* should have academic, vocational, or employment goals. *Transitions* is flexible enough to be used in open enrollment, managed enrollment, or traditional programs.

What components does *Transitions* have?

Student's Book with self-study Audio CD

The Student's Book contains ten topic-based units. Each unit contains five skill-focused lessons: Lesson A focuses on listening; Lesson B focuses on grammar; Lessons C and D focus on reading; and Lesson E focuses on writing. A self-study Audio CD containing the audio for the Lesson A listening exercises is included in the back of the Student's Book. In the Student's Book, the material on the CD is indicated by an icon 💿.

mp3 files for the reading passages

The reading passages in the Student's Book are provided as mp3 files, which can be downloaded from www.cambridge.org/transitions

Teacher's Manual

The Teacher's Manual has four sections: (1) Lesson plan suggestions, (2) Lesson notes, (3) Answer key, and (4) Audio script. The Lesson plan suggestions identify objectives for each of the four lesson categories (listening, grammar, reading, and writing), tie the exercises in the Student's Book to the stages of a lesson – warm up, presentation, practice, evaluation, and application – and suggest general procedures for conducting each. The Lesson notes provide additional activities for each unit. The Answer key is for the exercises in the Student's Book, and the Audio script is for listening activities in the Students Book.

Workbook

The Workbook is a natural extension of the Student's Book. It has one page of exercises for each lesson in the Student's Book. Workbook exercises can be assigned in class, for homework, or as student support if a class is missed. Students can check their own answers using the answer key in the back of the Workbook. If used in class, the Workbook can extend classroom instructional time by 35 to 40 minutes per lesson.

Unit Organization

Each unit is made up of five lessons. The lessons are sequenced in the same order that people acquire language: first listening, then speaking, then reading, and finally, writing. The second lesson focuses on grammar in oral communication. The focus of each lesson is on one of the four skills (listening, speaking, reading, writing). However, activities using all of these skills are provided in each lesson. The lessons are described in detail below.

LESSON A Get ready

Lesson A, the opening lesson of a unit, focuses students on the topic of the unit. It has three main sections: *Talk about the pictures*, *Listening*, and *Discuss*.

Talk about the pictures provides questions and photos to encourage students to share what they already know about the topic and to stimulate discussion about specific aspects of the topic.

Listening provides students with an opportunity to develop their skills in understanding and in processing lectures. The accompanying exercises provide practice in determining the main ideas of the listening passage and in taking notes.

Discuss provides an opportunity for students to personalize the language by discussing how the topic relates to their own lives.

In Lesson notes (section 2 of the Teacher's Manual), a warm-up activity is provided for each Lesson A. These warm-up activities introduce and practice note-taking tips such as "write only important words" and "use abbreviations."

LESSON B Grammar

Lesson B presents and practices a specific grammar point or points. It has three main sections: *Grammar focus*, *Practice*, and *Communicate*.

Grammar focus presents the grammar point(s) in chart form.

Practice provides exercises that check comprehension of the grammar point(s) and provide guided practice.

Communicate provides an opportunity for students to personalize the language. It guides students as they generate original answers and conversations.

In Lesson notes (section 2 of the Teacher's Manual), a warm-up activity is provided for each Lesson B. The notes give ideas on how to introduce that lesson's grammar point(s).

LESSONS C and D Reading

Lessons C and D develop students' reading skills and expand their vocabulary. These lessons have three main sections: *Before you read*, *Read*, and *After you read*.

Before you read provides exercises to activate prior knowledge and encourage students to make predictions about what they will read.

Read provides a reading passage several paragraphs in length. The reading passage expands on the topic presented in Lesson A, Get Ready.

After you read provides three sets of exercises. The first set checks student understanding of the reading passage. The second set expands students' vocabulary by building awareness of word families, prefixes, suffixes, roots, and parts of speech. The third set practices students' summarizing skills.

In the Lesson notes (section 2 of the Teacher's Manual) for Units 1, 4, 5, 7, 9, and 10, there are expansion activities that focus on developing prereading skills.

LESSON E Writing

Lesson E provides writing practice within the context of the unit. It has three main sections: *Before you write*, *Write*, and *After you write*.

Before you write provides warm-up exercises that help prepare students for the writing. These exercises include some or all of the following: questions that activate the language students will need, questions that encourage discussion about the writing genre, a model for students to follow when they write, prompts for a discussion of the model, or questions or graphic organizers to help students plan their writing.

Write sets goals for the writing so that students can be focused as they write.

After you write provides opportunities for students to check their own work as well as share and react to each other's writing.

In the Lesson notes (section 2 of the Teacher's Manual) for Units 2, 3, 6, and 8, there are expansion activities that focus on transitions within and between paragraphs.

Class Time Guidelines

One-hour lesson

Steps of the lesson	Approximate times
Warm-up	5–10 minutes
Presentation	10–20 minutes
Practice	20–30 minutes
Evaluation	10–15 minutes
Application	15–20 minutes

Two-hour lesson

Lessons in the Student's Book can take up to two hours, depending on a variety of factors. Some of these factors are the skill focus of the lesson, the proficiency of students within that skill focus, and the amount of supplementing of the Student's Book that the teacher does.

Lesson objectives

- Introduce Ss to the topic.
- Find out what Ss already know about the topic.
- Preview the lesson by talking about the pictures.
- Develop listening skills.
- Develop note-taking skills.
- Apply key concepts to Ss' own lives.

Warm-up (books closed)

- Before class, write the lesson focus on the board.

  Topic: _____

- Begin class. Point to the topic on the board. Ask a question(s) to elicit what Ss already know about the topic. Use the question in Exercise 1A, or create one or more questions of your own.

Presentation (Books open)

1 Talk about the pictures

Exercise 1A

- Read the question(s) aloud.
- Elicit a few answers.

Exercise 1B

- Read the questions aloud.
- Direct Ss' attention to the photos. Elicit some answers.

▼**Teaching tip**

Exercises 1A and 1B can be done with the whole class, in small groups, or as partner work, as detailed below:

- Whole class: Write Ss' ideas on the board to refer to after listening to the audio program.

- Small groups: Assign roles (facilitator, note-taker, reporter) and have the reporter take notes to use for reporting back to the class.

- Partner work: One of each pair reports back to the class; two pairs exchange ideas; or each pair posts their ideas in the classroom. Ss then do a gallery walk and read all the ideas.

Practice

2 Listening

⊙ Exercise 2A Listen

- Read, or have Ss read, the questions in the book.
- Play or read the audio program (see audio script, pages 24–28).
- Elicit answers and write them on the board. Alternatively, have volunteers write them. Leave the answers on the board for later reference.
- Provide practice in note taking. Do the activity suggested below in *Lesson Notes*, Lesson A.

  Unit 1: Write only important words.

  Unit 2: Abbreviate by omitting vowels from the middle of words.

  Unit 3: Eliminate small connecting words.

  Unit 4: Abbreviate by using only the first three or four letters of a word.

  Unit 5: Listen for clue words.

  Unit 6: Abbreviate one-syllable words by using only the first and last letters of the word.

  Unit 7: Write important facts.

  Unit 8: Cite the source when you take notes on facts.

  Unit 9: Leave space to fill in important words that are missed.

  Unit 10: Make a note of unfamiliar vocabulary or concepts.

Exercise 2B Listen again.

- Direct Ss' attention to the note-taking form in their books. Give them time to review it. Answer any questions they may have.
- Play or read the audio program through the first piece of key information. Ss take notes in their books.
- Elicit the key information a S filled in.
- Play the rest of the audio program without interruption. Ss listen and complete the exercise.

Evaluation

Listen again. Check your answers.

- Read, or have Ss read, the instructions.
- Play the audio program again for Ss to check their notes. Ss make additions or changes as necessary.
- Have Ss partner and compare notes to see if each has all the key information.
- Check the key information with the class.

▼ **Teaching tip**

Checking key information can be done in one of the following ways:

- Either project or duplicate the form on the board. Elicit and write the key information on the form, or have volunteers come to the board and fill in different parts of the form.

- Refer Ss back to their answers from Exercise 2A on the board. Delete and/or expand on their answers as necessary.

- Provide Ss with the answer key (see Answer key, pages 15–23). They compare their notes to the answer key and make changes as necessary.

Application

Exercise 2C Discuss. Talk with your classmates.

- Put Ss into small groups or pairs and have them read the questions.
- Have Ss share their answers to the questions.
- Provide closure to the exercise.

▼ **Teaching tip**

Providing closure to a discussion exercise can be done in one of the following ways:

- Each small group or pair reports their answers to the class.

- Each small group creates a tally, graph, or chart that presents a profile of their group, and posts it for the class to review.

Follow-up

- Assign the Workbook exercises. Ss can do the exercises in class or independently outside of class as homework.

Lesson B *Grammar*

Lesson objectives
- Present the form, meaning, and use of the target grammar.
- Provide guided practice of the target grammar.
- Provide opportunities for Ss to personalize the target grammar.

Warm-up (books closed)
- Before class, write the lesson focus on the board.
  Grammar focus: _____
- Begin class. Provide examples of the target grammar. Use the suggestions in Lesson Notes, lesson B, or create examples of your own.

Presentation (Books open)

1 Grammar Focus
- Direct Ss' attention to the grammar chart. Then do one of the following:
  - Read the information aloud.
  - Have a volunteer read the information aloud.
  - Allow time for Ss to read the information themselves.
- Ask questions to check that Ss understood what they read. Answer any questions.

Practice

2 Practice

Exercise 2A Write.
- Direct Ss' attention to the instructions.
- Have a volunteer read aloud the first sentence and give the sample answer. Check that Ss know how to do the exercise.
- Ss complete the exercise individually. Walk around and help as needed.
- Check answers.
- Explain anything that Ss still do not understand or that you think needs further explanation.

▼ **Teaching tip**
Checking answers can be done in one of the following ways:
- Volunteers come to the board and write their answers (one volunteer for each item in the exercise).
- Elicit answers for each item and write them on the board.
- Pairs compare their answers and discuss those that differ.
- Provide Ss with the answer key (see Answer key, pages 15–23) and have them check their own answers.

Exercise 2B Talk with a partner.
- Direct Ss' attention to the exercise and read the instructions aloud.
- Model the task.
- Ss work with a partner or in small groups to discuss the questions. Walk around the room and help as needed.

▼ **Teaching tip**
Modeling how to do an exercise can be done in one of the following ways:
- A volunteer demonstrates how to do the exercise with you.
- Two volunteers demonstrate how to do the exercise with each other.

Evaluation

Write
- Read the instructions aloud.
- Have a volunteer read the example aloud.
- Ss do the exercise individually. Walk around and help as needed.
- Have volunteers write their sentences on the board (a different S for each sentence), and have other volunteers read them.
- Point to each sentence and ask *Is this correct?*
- Make corrections on the board as needed.

Application

3 Communicate

Exercise 3A Work with a partner or a small group.

- Direct Ss attention to the instructions.
- Model the task.
- Have Ss work with a partner or in small groups to complete the exercise. Walk around and help as needed.
- Have Ss share their ideas.

▼ **Teaching tip**

Ss can share ideas in one or more of the following ways:

- If partner work:
  - Individuals report their partner's ideas.
  - Individuals write their partner's ideas on the board.
  - Ss write their partner's ideas on a piece of paper and post the ideas in the classroom. Ss then do a gallery walk and read all the ideas.
- If group work:
  - One S in a group reports orally or writes his or her group's ideas on the board.
  - Ss in the group collaborate, write their ideas, and post them in the classroom. Ss then do a gallery walk and read all the ideas.

▼ **Teaching tip**

Student groupings can be set up in one of the following ways:

- Assign Ss a partner or put them in a small group.
- Have Ss select a partner or form a small group themselves.

Follow-up

Workbook

- Assign the Workbook exercises. Ss can do the exercises in class or independently outside of class as homework.

Lesson C and Lesson D Reading

<table>
<tr><td>

Lesson objectives
- Introduce Ss to the topic.
- Find out what Ss already know about the topic.
- Develop reading skills.
- Develop vocabulary skills.
- Develop summarizing skills.

</td></tr>
</table>

Warm-up (books closed)

- Before class, write the lesson focus on the board.

  Topic: _____

  Vocabulary: _____

  (topic-related, idioms, prefixes, word families, positive and negative adjectives, suffixes)

- Begin class. Point to the topic and ask a question(s) that elicits what Ss already know. Use one of the questions in the book or create one or more questions of your own.

- Write Ss' ideas on the board.

Presentation (books open)

1 Before you read

- Direct Ss' attention to the instructions. Do one of the following:
  - Read the instructions aloud.
  - Have a volunteer read the instructions aloud.
  - Allow time for Ss to read the instructions themselves.

- Do the activity suggested below in *Lesson Notes*, Lesson C or D.

  Unit 1 Lesson C: Skim for paragraph focus.

  Unit 4 Lesson D: Skim first and last paragraphs to identify connection.

  Unit 5 Lesson D: Skim for topic sentences.

  Unit 7 Lesson C: Scan for names of organizations.

  Unit 9 Lesson C: Skim first and last paragraphs to identify connection.

  Unit 10 Lesson C: Scan heads; skim paragraphs without a head and develop a head parallel to other heads.

▼ **Teaching tip**

Exercise 1 can be done with the whole class, in small groups, or as partner work as detailed below:

- Whole class: Write Ss' ideas on the board. Leave these ideas on the board for later reference.

- Small groups: Assign roles (facilitator, note-taker, reporter) and have the reporter take notes to use for reporting back to the class.

- Partner work: One in each pair reports back to the class, two pairs exchange ideas, and each pair posts their ideas in the classroom. Ss then do a gallery walk and read all the notes.

2 Read

- Read the instructions aloud.
- Have Ss read the passage silently.
- Have Ss share information.
- Read the passage aloud (see script on pages 24–28) or play the mp3 audio. Ss follow along in their books. Tell Ss to write any words or expressions they do not understand in their notebooks.
- Have Ss write the words or expressions they did not understand on the board. Point to and read each one. Provide, or elicit from Ss, an explanation of the words or expressions.

▼ **Teaching tip**

Ss can share information in one of the following ways:

- Refer Ss to the ideas on the board. Ask which ideas were in the reading. Circle those ideas and erase the others.

- Ask Ss to share one thing they remember from the reading.

3 After you read

Exercise 3A Check your understanding.

- Read, or have Ss read, the instructions aloud.
- Have volunteers each read a question. Make sure that Ss understand the questions.
- Answer any questions Ss may have.
- Ss complete the exercise individually or with a partner. Walk around and help as needed.
- Check answers.

Teaching tip

Checking individual S's reading skills can be done in any of the following ways:

- Individuals write answers to the comprehension questions (checks understanding).

- Individuals read their answers aloud (checks for reading miscues, e.g., substituting one word for another, inserting words not there, omitting words that are there, reversing the order of words in the text).

- Individuals read groups of words cued by the teacher (e.g., for the sentence "Students who have trouble speaking English can take an English conversation class," the cues would be (1) six words that tell who, (2) two words that tell action, and (3) four words that tell what (checks for fluency).

Practice

Exercise 3B Build your vocabulary.

Note: In some lessons, this exercise requires that Ss use a dictionary.

- Read, or have Ss read, the instructions aloud.
- Model the task by doing the first item in the exercise with the class.
- Ss complete the remaining items in the exercise individually or in pairs. Walk around and help as needed.

Evaluation

- Check answers.

Teaching tip

Checking answers can be done in one of the following ways:

- Volunteers come to the board and write their answers (one volunteer for each item in the exercise).

- Elicit answers for each item and write them on the board. Pairs compare their answers and discuss those that differ.

- Provide Ss with the answer key (see Answer key, pages 15–23), and have them check their own answers.

Application

Exercise 3C Summarize the reading.

- Focus Ss on the instructions and on the cues provided to help them summarize.
- Ss, working with a partner, restate orally the main points of the reading using the cues, and practice their summaries orally.
- Signal time for Ss to start developing a written summary. Walk around and help as needed.
- Check written summaries.

Teaching tip

Checking the written summaries can be done in one of the following ways:

- Two pairs compare their summaries.

- Pairs post their summaries in the classroom. Ss then do a gallery walk and read all the summaries.

- Collect the summaries to review and comment.

Follow-up

- Assign the Workbook exercises. Ss can do the exercises in class or independently outside of class as homework.

Lesson E Writing

Warm-up (books closed)

- Before class, write the lesson focus on the board.

  Lesson Focus: Write _____

  Unit 1: a résumé

  Unit 2: about personal strengths

  Unit 3: a summary

  Unit 4: a cover letter

  Unit 5: a thank-you note

  Unit 6: about small talk

  Unit 7: an advice column

  Unit 8: about criticism

  Unit 9: an essay for college admission

  Unit 10: an action plan for solving a problem

- Begin class. Point to the lesson focus on the board and ask a question(s) that elicits what Ss already know about the writing genre or topic. Use the questions in Exercise 1A, or create one or more questions of your own. Write Ss' ideas on the board.

Presentation (books open)

1 Before you write
Exercise 1A Talk with your classmates.

- Direct Ss' attention to Exercise 1A. Do one of the following: Read the instructions aloud, have a volunteer read the instructions aloud, or have Ss read the instructions themselves.

- Have students answer the questions in pairs or small groups. Assign roles (facilitator, note-taker, reporter) and have the reporter take notes to use for reporting back to the class.

- Ss share their ideas.

- Repeat this process for each of the remaining exercises in *1 Before you write.*

- Do the activity suggested below in *Lesson Notes,* Lesson E.

  Unit 2: Analyze example for topic sentence and supporting examples.

  Unit 3: Identify transition words in example.

  Unit 6: Write topic sentences for two paragraphs.

  Unit 8: Identify focus of each paragraph in example.

Practice

2 Write

- Read the instructions aloud.

- Direct Ss' attention to the model provided for the writing in the Student's Book. You can also use the model provided in the Workbook or create one of your own.

- Elicit information about the organizational structure of the model. Use the questions in the Student's Book, in the Workbook, or create questions of your own.

- Have Ss do the writing in class or assign as homework.

Evaluation

- Have Ss revise their writing. Give them more than one opportunity to do this.

3 After you write

Exercise 3A Check your writing.

• Read, or have Ss read, the instructions.

• Demonstrate the use of the checklist by using it to analyze the model in the Student's Book, in the Workbook, or in an example you have written.

• Explain that the items on the checklist are to help Ss check that they have completed the writing according to the model.

• Have Ss use the checklist to evaluate their writing. Walk around and help as needed.

• Allow time for Ss to revise their writing based on their answers to the checklist. Address any issues you noticed as you observed Ss writing.

Exercise 3B Share your writing with a partner.

• Assign, or let Ss select, a partner.

• Have Ss share their writing with their partner and react to their partner's writing. Walk around and help as needed.

• Provide feedback on Ss' writing.

Application

• Ask questions that help Ss reflect on where and when they might use the skills they have learned by doing the writing assignment. For example: *What skills did you use that you have used before? What new skills did you learn? Where and when do you think you will use these skills again?*

Follow-up

• Assign the Workbook activities. Ss can do the exercises in class or independently outside of class as homework.

Lesson notes

Unit 1 Selling yourself

Lesson A Get ready

2 Listening, page 3: Warm-up for note taking (between Exercises 2A and 2B)

- Write on the board: *Tip: Write only important words.*
- Dictate the following sentences and have Ss take notes using the tip: *Sacramento is the capital of California. / If you want to take a class for no credit, you must register as an auditor. / One characteristic of successful people is that they set goals.*
- Provide feedback on notes by eliciting and writing on the board the key words (those words in boldface) or the words that Ss eliminated.

Lesson B Participial adjectives

1 Grammar focus, page 4: Warm-up for grammar paradigm

- Write on the board: *When my students smile in class I think they are interested in what I am teaching. When they frown I think they are bored. Smiling students mean an interesting class. Frowning students mean a boring class.*
- Underline the participial adjectives: *interested*, *bored*, *interesting*, *boring*.
- Elicit or explain how they are the same and how they are different. (adjective ending in *-ing* is the cause or source of the emotion, e.g., interesting class – the class caused interest; adjective ending in *-ed* is the receiver of the emotion, e.g., interested students – the class caused students to be interested).

Lesson C Reading

1 Before you read, page 6: (after *Talk with your classmates*.)

- Give Ss three to five minutes to identify the purpose or main idea in each paragraph.

  1: purpose of goal setting
  2: definition of goal setting
  3: focus on future
  4: key characteristics of goal setting
  5: adding detail
  6: measuring progress
  7: challenging but realistic
  8: completion date

Unit 2 Building self-confidence

Lesson A Get ready

2 Listening, page 13: Warm-up for note taking (between Exercises 2A and 2B)

- Write on the board: *Tip: Use abbreviations. One way to abbreviate is to omit vowels from the middle of words.*
- Write these words on the board and have Ss write the abbreviations:

background	(bkgrnd)	*clean*	(cln)
teacher	(tchr)	*bookkeeper*	(bkkpr)
junior	(jr)	*problem*	(prblm)

Lesson B The present passive

1 Grammar focus, page 14: Warm-up for grammar paradigm

- Write on the board: *Taking English classes improves your English. Your English is improved by taking English classes.*
- Elicit, or explain, the difference between the two sentences. (The first, active, focuses on the doer of the action. The second, passive, focuses on the result of the action.)

Lesson E Writing

2B Write, page 21

- Have Ss analyze the example by answering these questions: *What is the topic sentence?* (I am enthusiastic.) / *How many supporting examples does the writer give?* (5) / *What are they?* (1. I was always in a good mood. 2. I did my job well. 3. I was motivated. 4. I was friendly to the customers. 5. I made them feel comfortable.)

Unit 3 Volunteering

Lesson A Get ready

2 Listening, page 23: Warm-up for note taking (between Exercises 2A and 2B)

- Write on the board: *Tip: Eliminate small connecting words like* is, are, was, were; a, an, the; *and pronouns such as* they, these, his, that, *or* them.

- Dictate these sentences and have Ss take notes using the tip: *There was a huge **earthquake** in **Central America** last week. **Dozens** of people were **killed** and **hundreds** more were **injured**. **Many buildings** were **damaged** and **some** were totally **destroyed**.*
- Provide feedback on the notes by eliciting and writing on the board the key words (those words in boldface).

Lesson B Indirect (reported) speech

1 Grammar focus, page 24: Warm-up for grammar paradigm (books closed)

- Ask a student *What are you good at?*
- Write the answer and the reported speech version on the board, e.g., *I am good at making things. Carlos said that he was good at making things.*
- Underline verbs and elicit, or explain, the difference between the two sentences. (In the second sentence, the word *that* is used and the verb form has changed from present to past.)

Lesson E Writing

1D Read, page 31

- Tell Ss that transition words and phrases establish connections between ideas. They may indicate more information (*besides*, *in addition*), a cause or reason (*due to*, *because*), or an example (*for example*, *specifically*). They are also used to compare or contrast (*likewise*, *on the other hand*), and to conclude (*to summarize*, *given these facts*). Repetition of key words can also serve as a transition.
- Have Ss identify the transition words in the example summary and give the purpose of each. (1. *First* indicates that a list will follow. 2. *In contrast* compares or contrasts. 3. *Finally* indicates that the end of a list is nearing. 4. *The report concluded* indicates the conclusion.)

Unit 4 Effective job applications

Lesson A Get ready

2 Listening, page 33: Warm-up for note taking (between Exercises 2A and 2B)

- Write on the board: *Tip: Use abbreviations. One way to abbreviate is to write only the first three or four letters of a word.*
- Write these words on the board and have Ss write the abbreviations:

especially	(esp)	*subject*	(subj)
elementary	(elem)	*mathematics*	(math)
activity	(act)	*language*	(lang)

- Provide feedback on notes by eliciting and writing on the board the abbreviated forms.

Lesson B Past perfect

1 Grammar focus, page 34: Warm-up for grammar paradigm (books closed)

- Write on the board: *Lynn taught English in Japan in 1980. Lynn got her ESL teaching credential in 1985. Lynn had taught English in Japan before she got her ESL teaching credential.*
- Underline the verbs and elicit, or explain, how the third sentence is different from the first two. (In the third sentence, the verbs show that one action [had taught] happened before the other action [got].)

Lesson D Reading

1 Before you read, page 38: (after *Talk with your classmates*)

- Tell Ss that there is usually a connection between the first and last paragraphs of a reading passage.
- Have Ss read the first and last paragraphs to answer these questions: *The last paragraph refers to "these guidelines." What are they called in the first paragraph?* (ten tips) / *What two kinds of job applications does the writer talk about in the first paragraph?* (a neat application that catches the eye and a messy application that ends up in the trash) / *What two statements does the writer make in the last paragraph to encourage the reader to follow the tips?* (1. A potential employer is more likely to read your application from beginning to end. 2. It increases your chances of getting a job.)

Unit 5 Successful interviews

Lesson A Get ready

2 Listening, page 43: Warm-up for note taking (between Exercises 2A and 2B)

- Write on the board: *Tip: Listen for clue words.*
- Explain that clue words indicate that important information is forthcoming. For example, words like *benefits*, *advantages*, and *disadvantages*; words that signal organization, such as *first*, *next*, and *in conclusion*; or words that indicate level of importance, such as *above all* and *the most important*.
- Dictate these sentences and have Ss write the clue words: *There are **three reasons** for developing note-taking skills. **First of all**, they help you remember. **Another reason** is that people speak faster than they write. **Above all**, they help you stay focused.*
- Provide feedback on notes by eliciting and writing on the board the clue words (those words in boldface).

Lesson B Past modals

1 Grammar focus, page 44: Warm-up for grammar paradigm (books closed)

- Write on the board: *Ann felt sick. She went to work anyway, and now she has a high fever. She should have stayed home.*
- Ask students: *Did she go to work?* (Yes) / *How do you think she feels now?* (Terrible) / *Do you think she regrets going to work?* (Yes)
- Explain that *should have / shouldn't have* + past participle shows that the speaker regrets something he or she did or did not do in the past.
- Explain that these modals can be used to give advice about something in the past. Ask *What advice can you give Ann now?* (You should have taken some aspirin.)

Lesson D Reading

1 Before you read, page 48: (after *Talk with your classmates*)

- Give Ss three to five minutes to identify the topic sentence, or main idea, of each paragraph.

  1: Is there anything more you can do to improve the odds of getting the position?

  2: How do you make yourself stand out from the crowd?

  3: You must follow up.

  4: Sending a thank-you note after your meeting can help you make the most of your interview.

  5: A thank-you note is appropriate whether or not you felt the interview was successful.

  6: Write the note soon after the interview.

  7: It is important to send only *one* follow-up e-mail or note.

  8: Don't focus on what could have been, but on what may still lie ahead.

Unit 6 Small talk

Lesson A Get ready

2 Listening, page 53: Warm-up for note taking (between Exercises 2A and 2B)

- Write on the board: *Tip: Use abbreviations. For words that have only one syllable, write just the first and last letters.*
- Write these words on the board and have Ss write the abbreviations:

book	(bk)	weight	(wt)
quart	(qt)	word	(wd)
pint	(pt)	foot	(ft)

- Provide feedback on notes by eliciting and writing on the board the abbreviated forms.

Lesson B Tag questions

1 Grammar focus, page 54: Warm-up for grammar paradigm (books closed)

- Write *Where are you from?* on the board.
- Elicit an answer and write it on the board. (I am from Haiti.)
- Write two examples of tag questions about the S on the board, one true and one not true. Underline the *be* verbs in each. (Example 1: She is from Haiti, isn't she? / Yes, she is. / Example 2: She isn't from Mexico, is she? / No, she isn't.)
- Elicit, or explain, which is true and which is not and the difference in the *be* verb in each. In the first example, the sentence is true, and the *be* verb in the main clause is affirmative (but the tag is negative). In the second example, the sentence is not true, and the *be* verb in the main clause is negative (but the tag is affirmative).

Lesson E Writing

1 Before you write, page 61: (between Exercise 1D and 2 Write)

- Have Ss develop two topic sentences, one for a paragraph on similarities and one for a paragraph on differences. (e.g., There are several small-talk topics that are appropriate in both the United States and my home country. On the other hand, many small-talk topics appropriate in my home country are not appropriate in the United States.)

Unit 7 Improving relationships

Lesson A Get ready

2 Listening, page 63: Warm-up for note taking (between Exercises 2A and 2B)

- Write on the board: *Tip: Write important facts.*
- Dictate these sentences and have Ss take notes on the facts. *The average **lecturer speaks** approximately **125 to 140 words per minute**. / The average **note-taker writes** at a rate of about **25 words a minute**. / The average **person in the U.S.** spends **52 minutes** each **day reading** the **newspaper**.*
- Provide feedback on notes by eliciting and writing on the board important facts (those words in boldface).

Lesson B Unreal conditionals

1 Grammar focus, page 64: Warm-up for grammar paradigm (books closed)

- Elicit a few things that Ss would like changed in their community, the country, or the world. (e.g., Schools don't have enough money for their programs.)

- Have Ss provide one solution for each problem. (e.g., The government should spend more on education.)
- Rewrite each solution as an *if*-clause and underline *if* and the verbs (If the government spent more on education, schools <u>would have</u> enough money for their programs.)
- Elicit or explain the verb form shift. (The problem / condition: Schools don't have enough money; The solution: The government should spend more on education.) In the *if*-sentence version of the solution (. . . schools would have enough money . . .), the verb has changed from present (*don't have*) to *would* + base form. In the *if*-clause of the solution (If the government spent more . . .), the verb has changed from modal (*should* + base form) to simple past (*spent*).

Lesson C Reading

1 Before you read, page 66: (after *Talk with your classmates*)

- Remind Ss about what scanning involves.
- Have Ss scan the article to answer these questions: *What three organizations are cited and what are they cited for?* (Randstad USA – for a survey they did of 1,500 U.S. employees; Skillsoft – for an earlier survey; EEOC – government agency in charge of enforcing laws against discrimination)

Unit 8 Giving and receiving criticism

Lesson A Get ready

2 Listening page, 73: Warm-up for note taking (between Exercises 2A and 2B)

- Write on the board: *Tip: Cite the source when you take notes on facts.*
- Dictate these sentences and have Ss take notes, including both the facts and the sources: *According to the organization Small Business Management, most of us spend about 75% of our waking hours communicating our knowledge, thoughts, and ideas to others. / According to the Academic Skills Center, research shows that individuals can recall only 50% of what they hear, and 20 to 30% of what they recall is incorrect. / According to a U.S. government study conducted in 2003, between 21 & 23% of the adult population in the U.S. can't read well enough to fill out an application.*
- Provide feedback on notes by eliciting and writing on the board the important facts and their source (those words in boldface).

Lesson B Conditional clauses

1 Grammar focus, page 74: Warm-up for grammar paradigm (books closed)

- Write on the board: *Andre can't remember anything about the lecture. If Andre had taken notes during the lecture, he would have remembered what it was about.*
- Ask *Did Andre take notes during the lecture? What happened? What would have been different if he had taken notes during the lecture?*
- Elicit, or explain, that the *if*-clause expresses opinions or wishes about situations that were unreal (not true) in the past.

Lesson E Writing

1B Read, page 80

- Have Ss analyze the example by identifying the focus of each paragraph.
  1: where and when the story takes place
  2: situation in which the writer was criticized
  3: writer's actions as a result of the criticism
  4: lesson the writer learned

Unit 9 The right attitude

Lesson A Get ready

2 Listening, page 83: Warm-up for note taking (between Exercises 2A and 2B)

- Write on the board: *Tip: Leave space to fill in important words that you missed.*
- Dictate these sentences, covering your mouth or mumbling the words that are in boldface so that Ss miss some words. Have Ss take notes using the tip: *Estimates of the prevalence of dyslexia in the general U.S. population range from 5% to 20%. / We are about one centimeter taller in the morning than at night because cartilage in the joints gets compressed during the day. / The staple food of the Kanemba, a tribe living in Africa, is algae. They harvest Spirulina from lakes and use it to make a spicy cake.*
- Provide feedback on notes by eliciting from Ss questions they might ask to get the important words they missed (those words in boldface).

Lesson B Adverb clauses of concession

1 Grammar focus, page 84: Warm-up for grammar paradigm (books closed)

- Write on the board: *Although Mrs. Cheerful has a stressful job, she always has a smile on her face.*
- Point to *Although* and tell Ss that the *although* clause gives information that adds a surprising contrast (stressful job / always has a smile).
- Write on the board: *Mrs. Cheerful always has a smile on her face although she has a stressful job.*
- Ask if this sentence has the same meaning and punctuation as the previous sentence. (The same meaning, but there is no comma.)
- Finally, write on the board: *Even though Mrs. Cheerful has a stressful job, she always has a smile on her face.*
- Ask if this sentence has the same meaning as the previous sentence. (Yes)
- Explain that sometimes *even though* can be more emphatic than *although*.

Lesson C Reading

1 Before you read, page 86: (after Talk with your classmates)

- Remind Ss that there is usually a connection between the first and last paragraphs of a reading passage.
- Have Ss read the first and last paragraphs to identify the connection. (first paragraph: idyllic world turned upside down; last paragraph: because of attitude in dealing with problem positive things happened)

Unit 10 Writing at work and school

Lesson A Get ready

2 Listening, page 93: Warm-up for note taking (between Exercises 2A and 2B)

- Write on the board: *Make a note of key unfamiliar vocabulary or concepts. If repeated, they are key.*
- Dictate these paragraphs emphasizing the word(s) in boldface. Have Ss note the repeated unfamiliar vocabulary, guessing at spelling enough to ask a follow-up question about the word noted: *Dysarthria is a motor-speech disorder. Some people with dysarthria have limited tongue, lip, and jaw movement. A person with dysarthria may have slurred speech or a slow rate of speech. / Aphasia is a language disorder. Some people with aphasia have trouble using words and sentences (expressive aphasia). Some have problems understanding others (receptive aphasia). Others with aphasia struggle with both using words and understanding (global aphasia).*

- Provide feedback on notes by eliciting from Ss follow-up questions they might ask to get more information about the key unfamiliar vocabulary or concepts (those words in boldface).

Lesson B Causative verbs

1 Grammar focus, page 94: Warm-up for grammar paradigm (books closed)

- Write on the board:

Donna paid a hairdresser to color her hair.	*Donna had a hairdresser color her hair.*
The father asked his son to wash the car.	*The father had his son wash the car.*
Alex persuaded Mike to go to the game.	*Alex got Mike to go to the game.*
The mother required her child to eat breakfast.	*The mother made her child eat breakfast.*

- Elicit, or explain, how the sentences are the same and how they are different. Similar: In each one, the subject (Donna, the father, Alex, and the mother) has someone else do something. They do not do it themselves. In these sentences, the person who does the action follows the verb. Different: The meaning and grammar differ slightly: *make . . . do* = require; *have . . . do* = ask or pay; *get . . . to do* = persuade. Grammar: with *get / got*, *to* comes between the verb and the person who does the action.

Lesson C Reading

1 Before you read, page 96: (after *Talk with your classmates*)

- Have Ss look at the article to identify the two heads. (Composing e-mail, Sending and forwarding e-mail)
- Have Ss skim the three opening paragraphs to identify the topic and create a head for that topic. (The importance of proper e-mail etiquette)

Lesson E Writing

1B Read, page 100: (between Exercises 1B and 1C)

- Have Ss identify these sections of the article:

Problem (paragraph 1)
Consequences (paragraph 2)
New procedures (paragraph 3)
Implementation (paragraph 4)

Unit 1 Selling yourself

Lesson A Get ready
Exercise 2A, page 3
1. Hard skills and soft skills
2. Soft skills

Exercise 2B, page 3
Topic: Two types of job skills
A. Hard skills
   1. *Definition:* Technical skills & knowledge needed to do a job
   2. *Examples:* Pharmacy tech – names of medications, use cash register, take messages
B. Soft skills
   1. *Definition:* Personal qualities, people skills
   2. *Examples:* Hardworking, motivated, reliable, enthusiastic; communicate well with classmates & co-workers; customers like & trust you
Conclusion: Soft skills: more important

Lesson B Participial adjectives
Exercise 2A, page 4
1. tiring
2. exciting
3. interested
4. motivating
5. thrilled
6. dedicated
7. frustrated
8. disappointed

Exercise 2B, page 5
1. annoyed / disappointed
2. disappointed
3. embarrassing
4. I was amazed / amused / bored / frightened.; I thought it was amazing / amusing / boring / frightening.
5. I think they are exciting / frightening.; I am excited / frightened by them.
6. a boring job

Lesson C Reading
Exercise 3A, page 7
1. making a decision about what you want to achieve
2. detailed, measurable, realistic, has a completion date
3. It will make the goal clearer.

4. to avoid failure, so it is achievable
5. They stop paying attention to the goal.

Exercise 3B, page 7
1. movement toward a goal
2. practical, achievable
3. to find the amount or size of something
4. difficult but interesting
5. complete, attain, accomplish

Lesson D Reading
Exercise 3A, page 9
1. d   3. a   5. c
2. f   4. b   6. e

Exercise 3B, page 9
1. *to please somebody deeply; impression (n.), impressive (adj.)*
2. have good relations; [no related words]
3. responsible, adult behavior; mature (adj.), immature (adj.)
4. loyal, devoted; commit (v.), commitment (n.)
5. think something is worthwhile; value (n.), valuable (adj.)
6. study or examine closely; analysis (n.), analytical (adj.)

Lesson E Writing
Exercise 1C, page 11
1. Renee Smith
2. Teacher's Assistant in a preschool
3. organized, hardworking, dedicated
4. Associate of Arts (AA) from Atlanta Metropolitan College, Atlanta, GA, and high school diploma from International High School, Atlanta, GA
5. Teacher's Aide at Little Angels Preschool, Athens, GA, from 2010 to the present and Tutor at Center for Autism, Athens, GA, from October 2009 through June 2010
6. By asking her for them.

Unit 2 Building self-confidence

Lesson A Get ready
Exercise 2A, page 13
1. A comparison of two people, one confident, the other not confident.
2. David is more confident because he is motivated and optimistic, and he enjoys taking on new challenges. When he makes a mistake, he thinks of it as a learning experience.

Exercise 2B, page 13
David
   Strengths: motivated, optimistic, enjoys new challenges, learns from mistakes
   Weaknesses: sometimes works too quickly
Sarah
   Strengths: smart, works hard
   Weaknesses: judges self negatively if makes mistake; worries not doing a good job; feelings easily hurt; unrealistic expectations > easily disappointed

Lesson B The present passive
Exercise 2A, page 14
1. P   3. A   5. P   7. A
2. P   4. P   6. A

8. *The supervisor encourages the employees to have a good attitude.*
9. Charles's professors often criticize him for being late.
10. Mr. Chung is discouraged by the economy from leaving his job.
11. Being more positive improves Hugo's job performance.
12. Kevin's hard work motivates Sun Mi.
13. Mr. Chu's résumé is improved by using the Internet.
14. Kevin is criticized by Carmela for being late.

Exercise 2B, page15

1. It discourages you from having negative thoughts about yourself.
2. It is located at the Counseling Center.
3. The workshop is offered to all University Hospital employees.
4. The workshop is scheduled for Saturday, October 12, from noon to 2:00 p.m.

Lesson C Reading
Exercise 3A, page 17

1. the inner belief in their ability to be successful, feeling good about themselves
2. parents, siblings, friends, and teachers
3. withdrawn, unmotivated, overly sensitive to criticism

Exercise 3B, page 17

1. c   3. b   5. a
2. e   4. d

6. motivated   9. stress
7. influence   10. criticism
8. succeed

Lesson D Reading
Exercise 3A, page 19

1. 2   3. 6   5. 1
2. 4   4. 5

Exercise 3B, page 19

1. *showing great care in performing a job or task*
2. dependable, trustworthy, able to be trusted
3. willing to help or work with others
4. bold and confident
5. able to make or think of new, original things or ideas

Unit 3 Volunteering

Lesson A Get ready
Exercise 2A, page 23

1. Volunteering
2. Learn about the world of work, meet wonderful people, feel good about helping them

3. Become a tutor, volunteer at a day-care center or nursing home, volunteer for organizations that build low-cost housing for people who don't have much money, remove graffiti, work at a food bank

Exercise 2B, page 23

1. *Reasons to volunteer*
   a. gain information about work
   b. meet interesting people
2. *Examples of volunteer jobs*
   a. tutor
   b. day-care center volunteer
   c. nursing home volunteer
   d. volunteer for organizations that build homes for people who don't have much money
   e. remove graffiti, work at food bank
3. *Overseas volunteer opportunities*
   a. language tutor
   b. volunteer in health clinic

Lesson B Indirect (reported) speech
Exercise 2A, page 24

1. *She said (that) volunteering was a wonderful way to gain experience for a job.*
2. She said (that) they had many different types of volunteer jobs.
3. She said (that) volunteers could work in a school, hospital, nursing home, or library.
4. She said (that) they didn't need volunteers at the animal shelter right now.
5. She said (that) it was a good idea to include volunteer experience on a résumé.
6. She said (that) they were looking for several people to help with beach clean-up this weekend.

Exercise 2B, page 25

1. *John said (that) he was not really interested in working with animals.*
2. He said (that) he preferred to work with adults.

3. He said (that) he liked to help elderly people.
4. He said (that) he was good at building and carpentry.
5. He said (that) he could do this, but he didn't want to do it for long periods of time.
6. He said (that) he lived too far from the food bank.

Lesson C Reading
Exercise 3A, page 27

1. Sarah is paid. Audrey volunteers. Sarah is the coordinator of the recycling program. She supervises four volunteers. Audrey helps collect and organize the material for recycling.
2. She thought it would be too much work.
3. The cafeteria uses recycled paper products. Plant waste is used as compost in the college's gardens.
4. She said that people needed to use the program and support it.

Exercise 3B, page 27

1. again   6. supervise
2. together   7. recycle
3. together   8. collection
4. over, above   9. combine
5. together   10. coordinator

Lesson D Reading
Exercise 3A, page 29

1. college students
2. They can get college credit; it can help satisfy college requirements; it looks great on their résumé
3. talk to his or her advisor
4. a requirement for students to do volunteer work in order to graduate
5. that you want to help others and that you are curious about the world around you

Exercise 3B, page 29

1. volunteer   6. *volunteering*
2. *student*   7. participant
3. helper   8. helper
4. graduate   9. graduate
5. participant   10. Studying

Lesson E Writing
Exercise 1C, page 30

1. *students can get college credit*
   a. *Volunteers need advisor's permission*
   b. information about work and number of hours
   c. work related to S's major
2. helps satisfy college requirements
3. helps in getting a job
   a. looks good on a résumé
   b. tells employer you want to help others and that you are curious about the world around you

Unit 4 Effective job applications

Lesson A Get ready
Exercise 2A, page 33

1. steps in the job search process
2. six steps: the first step, next, the third step, fourth, next, finally

Exercise 2B, page 33

Steps in finding a job

1. decide type of job you want
2. look for job in your area
   Best way: word of mouth
   Other ways: online, in newspaper, listing at campus career center
3. fill out job applications
   Places to find: online & at workplace
4. ask previous employers for references
5. write résumé
6. write cover letter
7. *Wait for an invitation for an interview*
   While you're waiting: keep studying, develop skills

Lesson B Past perfect
Exercise 2A, page 34

1. By the time Paul had heard about the job, the position was filled.
2. Before Mary got a work-study job on campus, she had never worked.

3. Isaac had worked for his family business before he started his own company.
4. When Carla graduated from high school, she had already gotten her first job.
5. Before Thomas started nursing school he had worked as a medical receptionist.
6. Petra's children had grown up and moved out by the time she got her first job.
7. When Richard arrived for his job interview, the interviewer had already gone to lunch.

Exercise 2B, page 35

1. *Before his interview at the employment agency, Sergei had talked to his friends about job possibilities.*
2. *He hadn't written a résumé.*
3. He had made a list of references.
4. He had asked his previous boss for a letter of recommendation.
5. He had attended a workshop on networking.
6. He hadn't created a personal Web site.
7. He had done research online.
8. He hadn't ordered business cards.
9. He had bought a new suit.

Lesson C Reading
Exercise 3A, page 37

1. those who use tricks and deception to get private information from people
2. They place false ads online.
3. social security, student ID, or bank account numbers, credit card information, mother's maiden name
4. do research to see if the company is real: phone, send an e-mail, or visit the office

Exercise 3B, page 37

1. *applicant, application*
2. legally, illegally
3. scam
4. experience
5. experience
6. honesty
7. honestly
8. dishonest
9. experience

10. scam
11. dishonestly / illegally
12. applicants

Lesson D Reading
Exercise 3A, page 39

1. F   3. T   5. F
2. F   4. T

Exercise 3B, page 39

1. b   3. a   5. e
2. d   4. c

6. go over   9. found out
7. fill out   10. ended up
8. figure out

Unit 5 Successful interviews

Lesson A Get ready
Exercise 2A, page 43

1. how to make a good first impression
2. be on time, smile, pay attention to your body language, learn people's names, focus all your attention on the person you're meeting

Exercise 2B, page 43

Topic: Rules for making a good first impression
Why first impressions are important

1. only 3 seconds to form first impression
2. almost impossible to change first impression

Rules

1. Be on time.
2. Smile.
3. Pay attention to body language.
4. Learn people's names.
5. Focus attention on person meeting.

Lesson B Past modals
Exercise 2A, page 44

1. *She should have researched the company before the interview.*
2. She shouldn't have worn casual pants and a T-shirt. (She should have worn . . .)
3. She shouldn't have arrived late. (She should have arrived early.)

4. She should have brought a list of references.
5. *She could have read about the company online.*
6. She could have worn a suit.
7. She could have left her house earlier.
8. She could have e-mailed her references before the interview.

Exercise 2B, page 45

1. *Sam should have talked to John about his problem.*
2. *He shouldn't have written an angry e-mail.*
3. Sam shouldn't have sent the e-mail to John.
4. John shouldn't have forwarded the e-mail to the whole office, including Ms. Shue.
5. John should have paid attention before hitting "Send."
6. Ms. Shue should have been sympathetic to Sam's problem.
7. Ms. Shue shouldn't have yelled at Sam in front of the whole office.
8. *Sam could have tried to talk to his boss again.*
9. Sam could have taken care of his problem after work.
10. John could have deleted Sam's e-mail.
11. Ms. Shue could have been more flexible.
12. Ms. Shue could have spoken to Sam privately.

Lesson C Reading
Exercise 3A, page 47

1. He should have left earlier; he should have put his résumé in his bag; he should have learned how to pronounce the interviewer's name.
2. Sheila shouldn't have said negative things about her former co-workers.

3. Do: Prepare the materials you need ahead of time. Arrive early. Learn the name of the person who is interviewing you. Learn something about the company, school, or organization beforehand. Be honest about your skills, education, and experience. Be positive and interested. Follow up with a thank-you note. Don't: Wear inappropriate clothing. Ask about the salary right away. Be overly nervous. Speak negatively about others. Chew gum or smell like smoke. Act desperate for the position.

Exercise 3B, page 47

1. T 3. T 5. F
2. F 4. T

6. inappropriate
7. interviewee
8. desperate
9. scenario
10. flustered

Lesson D Reading
Exercise 3A, page 49

1. It is a great way to remind the interviewer that you are truly motivated and interested. It also shows that you have good manners.
2. If you send more than one, you will become an annoyance.

Exercise 3B, page 49

1. d 3. e 5. b
2. c 4. f 6. a

7. improve the odds
8. went well
9. stood out from the crowd
10. moved on
11. make the most of
12. Chances are

Unit 6 Small talk

Lesson A Get ready
Exercise 2A, page 53

1. to break the ice and to fill in the time before the start of an event

2. Appropriate topics: the weather, sports, your native country, your language, your family, traveling, learning English, movies, music, entertainment; Inappropriate topics: things Americans consider to be private – religion, politics, sex, and money; negative comments about people's bodies

Exercise 2B, page 53
Topic: Small talk
Definition: casual or "light" conversation about neutral or noncontroversial subjects
   Examples: weather or sports
Purposes
   1. to break the ice
   2. to fill in the time before the start of an event
Appropriate topics: the weather, sports, your native country, your language, your family, traveling, learning English, movies, music, entertainment

Inappropriate topics: things Americans consider to be private – religion, politics, sex, money; negative comments about people's bodies

Lesson B Tag questions
Exercise 2A, page 54

1. *wasn't it? / Yes, it was.*
2. doesn't she? / *No, she doesn't.*
3. wasn't he? / Yes, he was.
4. has she? No, she hasn't.
5. aren't you? / Yes, I am.
6. was it? / No, it wasn't.
7. are you? / Yes, I am,

Exercise 2B, page 55
Student A

1. You're from _____, aren't you?
2. You came to the United States last year, didn't you?
3. You're married, aren't you?
4. You have two children, don't you?
5. You didn't come to class yesterday, did you?
6. You're going to work right after class, aren't you?
7. You can't speak Spanish, can you?
8. You'll be in class tomorrow, won't you?

Student B

1. You're from ___, aren't you?
2. You just bought a car, didn't you?
3. You aren't married, are you?
4. You have a dog, don't you?
5. You didn't go to work yesterday, did you?
6. You're going to move to ___, aren't you?
7. You can't sing, can you?
8. You're leaving early today, aren't you?

Lesson C Reading
Exercise 3A, page 57

1. He was unaware of the difference between the speaker's words and their intentions.
2. How are you? Let's get together. Let's keep in touch. I'll call you. Let's talk soon.
3. Fine, thanks.

Exercise 3B, page 57

1. keep on walking / *continue* (to walk)
2. talk about seeing / discuss (seeing)
3. be guilty of lying / responsible for (lying)
4. be interesting in knowing / like to (know)
5. look forward to meeting / anticipate (meeting)

Lesson D Reading
Exercise 3A, page 59

1. Prepare a list of neutral conversation starters that you can call on in any situation.
2. Are you a student? What are you studying? Where are you going to school?
3. [Answers will vary.]

Exercise 3B, page 59

1. fit in / *be accepted by the people you're with*
2. call on / pull or recall from a resource
3. focus on / direct attention to
4. follow up / find out more about
5. write down / record
6. start up / begin

Unit 7 Improving relationships

Lesson A Get ready
Exercise 2A, page 63

1. people working together as a group
2. It makes it easier to accomplish goals.
3. It's easier and faster to complete tasks when people with different strengths and abilities work on them. People feel more invested when other people depend on them. Teamwork leads to greater involvement and lower absenteeism.

Exercise 2B, page 63

Topic: Teamwork

Definition: people working together as a group

Importance

   For organizations: easier & faster to complete tasks

   For individuals: more invested bec. people depend on you

Benefits

   1. Increased employee / student involvement

   2. reduced absenteeism

   3. learn valuable skills, e.g., conflict resolution, how to come to a consensus

   4. team members more adaptable & flexible

Conclusion

   In the past: American society encouraged individuals to act independently.

   Today: org. recognize value of people working together

Lesson B Unreal conditionals
Exercise 2A, page 64

1. *worked, might save*
2. would be, had
3. could concentrate, talked
4. were, wouldn't have
5. might be, trusted
6. were, would join
7. were, wouldn't force, would allow

Exercise 2B, page 65

1. If he didn't speak softly / If he spoke more loudly, the students could hear him.
2. If he asked questions, the students would pay attention.
3. If he used interesting examples, his lectures would not be boring.
4. If the students respected him, they would not come to class late.
5. If there were rules for behavior, the students would not use their cell phones and text during class.
6. If his tests were not easy / If his tests were hard, the students would be challenged.
7. If his department chair observed his class, she would know about the problems.

Lesson C Reading
Exercise 3A, page 67

1. Gossiping, wasting company time with poor time-management skills, leaving messes in common areas, unpleasant scents, loud noises, overuse of phones and laptops in meetings, misuse of company e-mail
2. A manager who repeatedly criticizes workers in front of their co-workers
3. [Answers will vary.]
4. Inappropriate touching or sexual remarks and using threats to force unwanted sexual activity on an employee or fellow student.

Exercise 3B, page 67

1. gossiping / *a comma between two nouns ("gossiping" and "passing") / the passing around of rumors and intimate information*
2. pet peeves / Other . . . included / gossiping, wasting company time, leaving messes in common areas, etc.
3. common areas / such as / lunch or meeting rooms
4. misuse of company e-mail / for example / e-mailing too often or copying too many people on messages

5. abusive behaviors / like / bullying and sexual harassment
6. bullying / is defined as / behavior done by a person with greater power for the purpose of intimidating, or frightening, a weaker or less powerful person
7. intimidating / or / frightening
8. sexual harassment / – which includes . . . – / inappropriate touching or sexual remarks and using threats to force unwanted sexual activity on an employee or fellow student

Lesson D Reading
Exercise 3A, page 69

1. It can put you in a bad mood, increase your stress level, and make you say things that you might regret later.
2. addressing the problem head on, that is, speaking to the person about the problem
3. talking about your feelings about a situation instead of the other person's actions. For example: "I would appreciate your keeping your voice down a little" instead of "You talk so loud, I can't hear myself think."
4. [Answers will vary.]

Exercise 3B, page 69

1. *drive you nuts / To irritate or annoy very much*
2. drive you up a wall / annoy you so much that you cannot do or think about anything else
3. in a bad mood / upset, unhappy, bad-tempered
4. turning a blind eye / choosing not to notice or react to something
5. address a problem head on / address it directly
6. clear the air / talk to someone about a problem in order to return to a good relationship
7. take into account / consider
8. grate on your nerves / make you very annoyed or irritated
9. make a big deal out of something / to exaggerate the seriousness or importance of something minor

Lesson E Writing
Exercise 1C, page 70

1. She names the problem and makes a sympathetic statement about the situation
2. two
3. *If I were you I would* . . . and imperative verbs: *Try to* . . . , *Explain* . . . , *Ask* . . .)

Unit 8 Giving and receiving criticism

Lesson A Get ready
Exercise 2A, page 73

1. Ray's professor / for doing poorly on a test / He wrote a negative comment on Ray's paper.
2. Ray was angry. He slammed the door on the way out of his professor's office. Three weeks later he dropped out of school.
3. Negative criticism can have terrible consequences. Constructive criticism gives solutions.

Exercise 2B, page 73

Topic: Giving constructive criticism
Ray's story
   Test grade: F
   Professor's written comment: "Disappointing performance"
   Comments to Ray in office: not trying hard enough, should think about quitting school.
   Ray's reaction: angry; slammed door; dropped out of school.
Consequences of negative criticism:
1. makes people angry
2. causes people to lose confidence & motivation
How to give constructive criticism:
1. Say something good about the person.
2. Talk about mistakes & solutions to problem.
3. Offer another positive statement.

Lesson B Conditional clauses
Exercise 2A, page 74

1. *had received, would have gone*
2. wouldn't have been, had remembered
3. would have gotten, had turned in
4. had written, wouldn't have made
5. hadn't yelled, wouldn't have gotten
6. wouldn't have finished, hadn't helped
7. had had, would have had

Exercise 2B, page 75

1. *If the boss hadn't trusted Mario, he wouldn't have assigned him an important project.*
2. If the project hadn't had a tight deadline, Mario wouldn't have worried about finishing on time.
3. Mario would have felt (more) confident if he had had a colleague to consult.
4. Mario wouldn't have needed to work overtime if there hadn't been problems.
5. If Mario's desk hadn't been full of papers, he wouldn't have lost an important document.
6. If Mario's computer hadn't crashed, he wouldn't have lost any data.
7. Mario wouldn't have finished the project on time if he hadn't stayed up all night.
8. The boss wouldn't have been pleased if Mario hadn't finished the project on time.

Lesson C Reading
Exercise 3A, page 77

1. like an animal under attack
2. to avoid defensive emotions, which may make people get more rigid and listen less
3. show that you heard the criticism; ask for more information; try to find something both parties can agree on; respond to the criticism
4. [Answers will vary.]

Exercise 3B, page 77

1. *verb*
2. adjective
3. verb
4. adjective
5. adverb
6. whole sentence

Lesson D Reading
Exercise 3A, page 79

1. That he needed to stop chitchatting so much with his co-workers because he wasn't working fast enough.
2. His heart started racing, and all he could think about was how bad it made him feel.
3. He would have been more prepared, and he would have been more calm.
4. He's going to e-mail Bill an apology, ask for another meeting, and get back to work.

Exercise 3B, page 79

1. *no*
2. make a mistake
3. become upset or angry
4. talk
5. talk too much
6. contribute the same amount as everyone else; do one's share of the work
7. lose one's temper; get very angry

Lesson E Writing
Exercise 1C, page 81

1. In Paris during the summer after the writer graduated from high school.
2. A waiter; he laughed at her accent; it was negative.
3. She was devastated. She was so flustered she couldn't remember another word in French.
4. For several days she refused to speak French.
5. She could have laughed at herself.
6. She started listening to the way French people speak and trying to imitate their accent, and she began to speak French again. She learned not to let people's comments about her accent bother her.

Unit 9 The right attitude

Lesson A Get ready
Exercise 2A, page 83

1. the instructor of a workshop; people taking the workshop; they want to adjust their attitude for success.
2. Positive people are upbeat and cheerful; they smile a lot; they support their teammates; they shine a light on other people's accomplishments; they rarely complain. Negative people don't smile or laugh very much; they always seem unhappy; they are often critical or sarcastic; they tend to be more focused on themselves than on others.

Exercise 2B, page 82

Topic: Adjusting your attitude for success

Behaviors of positive people: upbeat, cheerful, smile a lot, try to do best, support teammates, shine a light on other people's accomplishments, rarely complain

Behaviors of negative people: don't smile or laugh much, seem unhappy, often critical or sarcastic, tend to be focused on selves, complain

Lesson B Adverb clauses of concession
Exercise 2A, page 84

1. *Although Mike has a great job, he complains about his work all the time.*
2. Susan still feels stressed out even though she goes to stress reduction classes.
3. Although John is a positive example for his staff, some people still complain about him.
4. Even though Sam's teacher helped him a lot, Sam decided to transfer to another class.
5. Although Jim doesn't like his job, he stays because of the salary.
6. Peter got an A on the final exam even though the accounting class was very hard.

Exercise 2B, page 85

1. *Although Ms. Muse has a stressful job, she always has a smile on her face.*
2. Although / Even though Ms. Muse has too much work, she always helps other people.
3. Although / Even though she has a low salary, Ms. Muse doesn't complain.
4. Ms. Muse is never late although / even though she lives far away.
5. Although / Even though Ms. Muse has a sick mother, she never misses a day of work.
6. *Although / Even though Mr. Grimes has an easy job, he never smiles at anybody.*
7. Mr. Grimes never helps others although / even though he has lots of time.
8. Although / Even though Mr. Grimes has a good salary, he says it's not enough.
9. Mr. Grimes is often late although / even though he lives near the office.
10. Although / Even though Mr. Grimes has no family responsibilities, he is often absent from work.

Lesson C Reading
Exercise 3A, page 87

1. invasive prostate cancer
2. He persevered and he had a positive attitude.
3. volunteering with charities to help raise awareness about cancer

Exercise 3B1, page 87

1. idyllic / P / *happy, normal*
2. invasive / N / needed immediate surgery
3. setback / N / can't surrender, give up
4. persevere / P / keep going
5. stunned / N / upset
6. anxiety / N / helped him deal
7. determined / P / get back to his job
8. adored / P / enjoyed
9. focused / P / a job he loved
10. count (one's) blessings / P / positive things, lucky

Lesson D Reading
Exercise 3A, page 89

1. a disease
2. difficulties in childhood or personal lives, response to unfair treatment
3. absenteeism, accidents, employee mistakes, theft
4. avoid negative co-workers, think and speak positively, don't participate in office gossip, acknowledge good work and be generous with compliments, seek positive solutions to problems
5. No, if looking at medical science, but yes in the sense that, like a cold, it is contagious

Exercise 3B, page 89

1. -itis / negativitis / noun / illness of negative thinking
2. -ity / negativity / noun / a bad, unpleasant, critical, or disagreeing attitude
3. -ist / psychologists / noun / people who study the psyche, or mind
4. -ism / absenteeism / noun / habit of being absent, especially from work or school
5. -hood / childhood / noun / the time when a person is a child
6. -ate / contaminate / verb / make bad, unpure; eradicate / verb / destroy, get rid of ; participate / verb / become involved in, take part in

Unit 10 Writing at work and school

Lesson A Get ready
Exercise 2A, page 93

1. because writing is a skill that transfers to almost any job
2. two-thirds of salaried workers do some kind of writing in their jobs; 20-35 percent of hourly workers have some writing responsibility; in the future, job seekers without writing skills won't get hired; workers without writing skills won't get promoted; companies today spend up to three billion dollars to improve workers' writing skills
3. take classes and practice

Exercise 2B, page 93

Introduction
> *Topic:* The importance of writing
> *Examples:* nursing assistants, daily progress reports on patients; automotive technicians, work orders for cars that need repairs; housekeepers, shopping lists

Importance of writing
> *1.* 2/3 salaried workers write on job
> *2.* 20–35% hourly workers write
> *3.* Future job seekers w/out writing skills won't get hired; workers w/out writing skills won't get promoted.
> *4.* Companies spend up to $3 billion to improve workers' writing skills.

Report's conclusions
> *1.* Today, writing as important as math & computer skills.
> *2.* Writing skills transfer to job.

How to improve your writing: Take classes & practice as much as possible.

Lesson B Causative verbs
Exercise 2A, page 94

1. *Mrs. Ramsey had her daughter answer the phone.*
2. The boss made everyone come in early.
3. Corina had a manicurist give her a manicure.
4. Ajay got a classmate to proofread his history paper.
5. The school made all the parents sign a consent form before the children's field trip.
6. Katarina got all her friends to read her blog.
7. The school had a gardener plant flowers in front of the building.
8. The city had a famous artist paint a mural on the new bridge.

Exercise 2B, page 95

1. *Dr. Brown made a student stay after school.*
2. Dr. Brown made the teachers come to an important meeting during their lunch hour.
3. Dr. Brown made her assistant retype a memo.
4. Dr. Brown had the janitor repair a broken window.
5. Dr. Brown had her assistant water the plants in her office.
6. Dr. Brown had some honor students show visitors around the campus.
7. Dr. Brown got some students to come to school on Saturday to paint over graffiti.
8. Dr. Brown got the parents' association to raise money for a new gym floor.
9. Dr. Brown got the mayor to visit the school.

Lesson C Reading
Exercise 3A, page 97

1. Say what the message is about in the subject line; keep e-mail formal until you are told that it's OK to use first names; keep the e-mail brief; use a friendly and respectful tone; use good manners; don't type in all capital or all lowercase letters; never gossip or fight in e-mail.
2. Wait to enter the address until after you write the e-mail; proofread; don't use "Reply all" unless you are sure everyone on the list needs to read the e-mail; ask permission to send a large attachment; if you forward an e-mail, identify yourself and say why you are forwarding it; don't send personal e-mails from work.
3. [Answers will vary].

Exercise 3B, page 97

1. innovative / *new, modern* / *old-fashioned*
2. savvy / smart, knowledgeable / ignorant, uninformed, uneducated
3. proper / correct / improper, wrong, inappropriate
4. vague / unclear / clear, precise

5. respectful / showing respect or regard / disrespectful, insulting, rude
6. private / intended for only one person / public
7. timely / quickly, soon / late

Lesson D Reading
Exercise 3A, page 99

1. Because time is short, business people often just skim. They don't have time to read everything in depth.
2. Keep it Short and Simple. Use short sentences and keep the language simple and familiar.
3. It tells the reader who is responsible for performing the action, and it is more interesting.

Exercise 3B, page 99

1. on top of / *informed about* / *at the highest point*
2. short / lasting only a small amount of time / not long or tall in distance
3. skim / read quickly for main ideas / get rid of a substance such as fat floating on the surface of a liquid

4. key / most important / instrument for locking or unlocking a door
5. crisp / clear, precise / fresh and crunchy
6. fuzzy / unclear, vague / covered with fine hairs
7. concrete / specific / hard material used for building roads or walls

Lesson E Writing
Exercise 1C, page 101

Problem: Students using cell phones to cheat on exams
Consequences:
1. Students who do not cheat are forced to compete unfairly against those who do.
2. Instructors who wish to prevent cheating must spend time and resources creating alternative versions of tests.
3. News about cheating on campus damages the reputation of the college in the community.

Recommendations:
1. Upon entering the exam room, students carrying cell phones must turn them off and leave them with the exam proctor at the front of the room.
2. Students will not be allowed to carry backpacks or heavy jackets to their seats.
3. In classes of 25 or more students, the college will hire additional proctors to supervise exams.
4. Students caught cheating will receive an automatic score of zero on the exam, and they will be required to attend a disciplinary meeting with the Dean of Students.

Schedule: [Answers will vary.]

Audio script

Unit 1 Lesson A

Exercise 2 Listening
Student's Book page 3, track 2

Good afternoon, everyone.

I understand that some of you will start looking for a job as soon as this course finishes, and others plan to get some more training first . . . maybe go to college or sign up for vocational classes . . .

So, today I want to talk about a topic that's very important for all of you, and that is the kinds of skills and qualities that you will need to get a job in today's competitive economy . . . Basically, there are two types of skills you will need if you want to be successful. The first type is called "hard skills," and the second type is called "soft skills."

"Hard skills" are the technical skills and the knowledge you need in order to do a job. These are things you can learn in school or on the job. For example, if you want to be a pharmacy technician, you will need to learn the names of medications, how to use a cash register, how to take messages from doctors, and so on. If your goal is to get a job in a factory, then you need to learn how to use the machines and maybe how to operate a computer. These are hard skills.

"Soft skills" are a little harder to define. They include your personal qualities and what we call your "people skills." For example, are you hardworking, motivated, reliable, and enthusiastic? Do you communicate well with your classmates and co-workers? Do customers like you and trust you? Those are examples of soft skills.

Sometimes people ask me what's more important, hard skills or soft skills. Well, both of them are important, but I think soft skills are probably more important, because they're harder to teach and because they are transferable . . . I mean, you can take them with you from job to job. If you have a good attitude and you communicate well, you will be successful in any job you have.

Unit 2 Lesson A

Exercise 2 Listening
Student's Book page 13, track 3

I'd like to describe two different workers for you, David and Sarah, and while I'm talking about them I'd like you to think about which one got a promotion. OK?

So, David and Sarah, they work together in a busy office. Both of them are dedicated to their jobs; they're conscientious and loyal, but their personalities are very different. David is a motivated, optimistic person who enjoys taking on new challenges. It's true that sometimes he works too quickly and makes mistakes, but when this happens, he thinks of it as a learning experience and promises himself that he'll do better next time.

All right, now Sarah, on the other hand, judges herself very negatively if she makes a mistake. Although she's really smart and works hard, she often worries that she is not doing a good job, and her feelings are easily hurt when anyone criticizes her. Sarah's expectations of herself are unrealistically high, so she's easily disappointed.

OK, so, which worker do you think got the promotion? David, obviously. He's happy and enthusiastic about his new responsibilities, while Sarah, yeah, as you can probably guess, feels like a failure.

Unit 3 Lesson A

Exercise 2 Listening
Student's Book page 23, track 4

The topic of our class today is volunteering, or working to help others without getting paid for it. According to the U.S. government, about 26 percent of Americans volunteer at least once a year, and I'm sure you know people who volunteer much more often, maybe even once a week.

If you've ever volunteered anywhere, then you know that volunteering can be a very beneficial experience. Although you don't earn money, you can learn a lot about the world of work. Volunteering can be a type of on-the-job training. Also, you can meet wonderful people and feel good about helping them.

There are all kinds of places to volunteer, and each place is looking for people with different abilities. If you are interested in working with children, you could become a tutor and help them with their homework, or volunteer in a day-care center. If you enjoy working with elderly people, you could volunteer your time in a nursing home. If you like building things, you could volunteer for an organization that builds low-cost housing for people who don't have much money. Other volunteer work you might be interested in could be, removing graffiti from public places, or working at a food bank to put together food boxes or baskets for low-income families.

Volunteer work can also take you overseas. If you're interested in working in other countries, you could become a language tutor or, if you have medical skills, you could volunteer to help in health clinics around the world, like so many doctors did following the earthquake in Haiti in 2010.

So whether you're volunteering to gain experience for a job or you just want to help others, there are many opportunities for you to be involved in your local community or the larger global community.

Unit 4 Lesson A

Exercise 2 Listening
Student's Book page 33, track 5

I know that some of you haven't ever had a job before, especially if you're a full-time student, so I thought I'd start our workshop today by giving you an overview of the main steps in the job search process. It can be a long process, so let me encourage you to stop by the campus career center anytime if you need help, OK?

OK. So the first step in finding a job is deciding what type of job you'd like to have. What are your interests? What are your hobbies? What are you good at? What kind of experience do you have? It's good to write these things down, and then ask yourself, "What kind of job fits my interests and abilities?"

Next, start looking for jobs in your area. One of the best ways to find out about job openings is by word of mouth – you know, through talking to friends, neighbors, and family members. Look online, and check out the listings at the campus career center. You can also look in the newspaper, of course.

The third step is filling out applications for the jobs you're interested in. For most jobs these days, you can find applications online, or else you can go to the workplace itself. Fill out the job application carefully and don't lie!

Fourth, if you're asked to give references, ask your previous employers to give you a recommendation. If you've never worked before, think of a trusted friend or teacher who knows you well and would be a good personal reference for you.

Next, you'll also need to write a résumé to send with your application. We'll talk about résumé writing at our next meeting.

Finally, depending on the type of job you are applying for, you may need to write a cover letter to send in with your job application and résumé. A personalized letter that tells an employer how much you are interested in the job could make all the difference in getting an invitation to come for an interview.

And speaking of interviews . . . the hardest thing, after you've done all the things we've just talked about, is waiting for the phone call asking you to come in for an interview. While you're waiting, make good use of your time. Keep studying and developing your skills. If you do these things, I promise that sooner or later you'll find a good job.

Unit 5 Lesson A

Exercise 2 Listening
Student's Book page 43, track 6

When people meet for the first time, how long do you think it takes them to form their first impression of each other? Five minutes? One minute? Would you believe . . . three seconds or less?

That's right, three seconds for someone to look you over and evaluate you when they meet you for the first time. And, research shows, once someone forms an opinion of you, there's almost nothing you can do to change their minds. So because first impressions are so important, in the next few minutes I want to give you five simple rules for making a great first impression, whether at work or in a social situation. Ready?

Rule number one in North American culture is – be on time. If your job interview is set for 9:00 a.m., try to get there early, at 8:45. If someone invites you for dinner for 7 o'clock, it's OK to arrive at 7:15, but any later than that and your host might think you are rude – and that's not the way to make a good first impression.

Rule number two, and again I'm talking about American culture, is – smile! A smile makes you seem warm and open, and research even shows smiling can improve your health and your mood. There's nothing like a smile to create a good first impression.

My third rule is – pay attention to your body language. Stand up straight, make eye contact, and greet your new acquaintance with a firm handshake. These behaviors will make you seem confident and attractive, and they will make it easy for people to remember you.

Rule number four is – learn people's names. If it's hard for you to pronounce a name, it's OK to ask the person to repeat it. And then, do your best to use the person's name during your first conversation. Doing this will give the impression that you are polite and truly interested in getting to know the other person.

And finally, focus all your attention on the person you're meeting. Have you ever been introduced to someone who, in the middle of the introduction, excused themselves to answer their cell phone? Remember, the person in front of you is always more important than the person calling you on the phone. If you want to make a good first impression, turn off your cell phone and give your new acquaintance 100 percent of your attention.

If you follow these five rules, I promise that you will make a good first impression on everyone you meet. Good luck!

Unit 6 Lesson A

Exercise 2 Listening
Student's Book page 53, track 7

I'd like to spend some time today talking about small talk. Now, I know this is a subject that many of you are very interested in, because the rules of conversation are quite different in your home cultures. Students are always asking me, "What is small talk? When do we do it, and why?" and "Which topics are OK to talk about?" So let me start by giving some general answers to those questions.

So, first of all, what is small talk? Well, it's a kind of casual or "light" conversation about neutral or noncontroversial subjects like the weather or sports. It's the kind of conversation we have with people in places like parties, or standing in line somewhere, or when we're waiting for a class or a business meeting to start.

One purpose of small talk is to "break the ice," which means to start a conversation with another person, especially a person you don't know very well. It's a polite way to start talking with someone, and often it's a bridge to talking about bigger topics later, when you feel more comfortable with each other. Another purpose of small talk is to fill the time before the start of an event like a meeting or a class.

OK, so let's say you're at a party with a bunch of people you don't know very well, and you need to make small talk. What should you talk about, and which topics should you avoid?

"Safe" topics include the weather and sports, as I said; also anything about your native country or your language, your family, traveling, or learning English. Movies, music, and entertainment are also good topics.

Now, inappropriate topics are things that Americans consider to be private, so religion, politics, sex, and money – you shouldn't ask questions about those things until you know people very well. You should never ask Americans how much money they make or what they paid for something. It's also inappropriate to make negative comments about people's bodies, like saying they've gained weight or that they look sick.

Remember, the purpose of small talk is to open up a conversation and to get to know another person. Don't start out by talking about subjects that are too personal or too heavy. If you approach another person with respect, and you are careful about the subjects you choose to speak about, people will feel comfortable around you. It's also a great way to practice your English!

Unit 7 Lesson A

Exercise 2 Listening
Student's Book page 63, track 8

The topic of my talk today is teamwork. If you've ever had a job interview, chances are that the interviewer asked you what teamwork means to you, or whether you're a team player, right? Well, what is teamwork, and why is it important?

Let's start with a definition: Teamwork means working together as a group, or team. A long time ago, we only used this word to talk about sports, like a baseball team, but these days it means any group of people who collaborate, I mean, who work and think together, to accomplish a common goal. Just a few examples are a team of workers working to find a way to reduce their company's use of electricity, or a group of students working together to design a park, or a group of volunteers who are working on a plan to raise money for their children's school.

Teamwork is important because it makes it easier to accomplish goals. Especially when you have a large project, it's easier and faster to complete the task when you have a team of people with different strengths and abilities working on different pieces of it. So teamwork benefits organizations, but it can also benefit individuals. If you work as a team at your job or school, you will feel more invested in what you are doing because other people on your team are depending on you.

Teamwork has other important benefits, too. According to research, organizations that use teamwork have better employee and student involvement and reduced absenteeism – fewer people missing work or school because of stress or illness. Additionally, when people work together in a group, they learn valuable skills such as conflict resolution and how to come to a consensus, or agreement. And workers or students involved in teamwork are more adaptable and flexible because they learn to work with people who have different work and study habits and styles.

For these reasons, teamwork is an essential part of today's society, in both the workplace and in academic settings. Traditionally, American society has encouraged individuals to act independently in order to rise up in the world, but these days more and more organizations are recognizing the value of people working together to reach common goals.

Unit 8 Lesson A

Exercise 2 Listening
Student's Book page 73, track 9

No one likes to receive criticism, right? And I'm sure all of us have been in situations where a boss or a teacher or a parent criticized us and we didn't respond well to the criticism. But just as important as knowing how to handle criticism is knowing how to give criticism that's fair and constructive, and that's the topic of my lecture today.

Let's look at the case of a student named Ray who was criticized by his professor. Last week Ray had an important exam. He studied as much as he could, but it wasn't enough, because when he got his exam back the first thing he saw was a big red F at the top of his paper. The professor had circled all the wrong answers in red and had written "Disappointing performance – See me in my office" at the bottom of the paper.

The professor didn't know that Ray is extremely busy because, in addition to his course load, he also works part-time. He usually has to stay up late at night to get his homework done, and lots of times he goes to bed at 2:00 a.m. after getting home from his restaurant job at 11:00 p.m.

Ray went to see his professor and tried to explain his situation, but the professor wasn't sympathetic. "You need to try harder," he said. "If you can't handle working and studying at the same time, maybe you should think about quitting school."

This made Ray so angry that he slammed the door on the way out of his professor's office. But then he started to think that maybe his professor was right. And three weeks later, he dropped out of school.

Now, what can we learn from this scenario? We see that negative criticism can have terrible consequences. It can make people angry and cause them to lose confidence and motivation.

If you have to criticize someone, experts say, do it constructively, or positively. Constructive criticism has three steps: First, say something good about the person or their work. This will help them relax and prepare them for the next step. In step two, talk to the person about their mistakes. Be honest, but be gentle. And don't stop there – talk to the person about solutions to the problem. The goal is to help a person learn and grow, not to hurt or embarrass them. Finally, in the third step, offer another positive statement about the person that lets them know you care about them. This will leave the person feeling motivated instead of discouraged. Imagine if Ray's professor had followed these steps. He might have been able to help Ray instead of causing him to drop out of school.

Unit 9 Lesson A

Exercise 2 Listening
Student's Book page 83, track 10

Welcome, everyone, to today's workshop, which we're calling "Adjusting Your Attitude for Success." As everybody knows, attitude affects all aspects of our lives – the people around us, the success of our work, and the enjoyment of our daily tasks. Whether you think you have a positive or a negative attitude, this class will help you to become more successful at work, at school, and at home. OK?

To begin, how do you recognize a positive person? Well, behavior can reveal a lot about a person's attitude. Positive people are generally upbeat and cheerful. They smile a lot, even if they're stressed out. They're usually inspired by their work and try to do their best. They have a "can-do" attitude, meaning they welcome challenges and believe that there's a solution to every problem. Positive people also support their teammates or co-workers. They like to shine a light on other people's accomplishments, and they rarely complain. In short, positive people are a pleasure to be around.

Now let's look at the opposite type of person, the person nobody wants to have on their team because of their negative attitude. How do they behave? Well, typically, negative people don't smile or laugh very much, and they always seem to be unhappy about something. They are often critical or sarcastic, and they tend to be much more focused on themselves than on others. They complain that no one wants to eat lunch with them, but they can't see that it's their own negativity that is pushing friends, family, and colleagues away. Do you know anybody like that?

Now these are extreme descriptions, of course. Nobody is totally positive or totally negative all the time. But if you feel there's too much negativity in your life and you'd like to take steps to fix it, this class will give you the skills you need to adjust your attitude for a better and more successful life. So let's get started.

Unit 10 Lesson A

Exercise 2 Listening
Student's Book page 93, track 11

OK, today I want to talk to you about the importance of writing. No matter what your future job is, chances are you will have to do some kind of writing. For example, nursing assistants have to write daily progress reports on their patients. Automotive technicians need to write work orders for cars that need repairs. Housekeepers have to write shopping lists.

To show just how important writing is, let me quote you some of the findings from a 2010 report by the National Commission on Writing for America's Families, Schools, and Colleges.

Number one: Two-thirds, that's more than 60 percent, of salaried workers in large American companies – that means full-time, career workers – have to do some kind of writing in their jobs.

Number two: Among hourly workers, between 20 and 35 percent of workers also have some writing responsibility.

Number three: Moving into the future, job seekers who cannot write well will probably not get hired, and workers who already have jobs may not get promoted if they don't have good writing skills.

Number four: Good writing skills are so important that the Commission found that companies spend up to three billion dollars a year on improving their workers' writing skills to make them more productive.

The Commission's conclusion was that in today's job market, writing skills are just as important as math and computer skills. Furthermore, if you learn to write well in school, it will transfer to almost any job, from taking orders in a restaurant to writing business reports for a company. But if you don't learn how to write well, you could end up with a low-paying job and have no options for promotion.

So if you want to improve your writing skills, take classes and practice writing as much as possible. And have patience. It takes time to learn how to write well, but if you practice regularly, you can learn how to write more clearly, accurately, and concisely.